The Phantom of the Opera

Gaston Leroux

Abridged and adapted by Mary Ansaldo

Illustrated by Karen Loccisano

A PACEMAKER CLASSIC

Globe
Fearon

Upper Saddle River,
New Jersey

Supervising Editor: Stephen Feinstein
Project Editor: Karen Bernhaut
Editorial Assistant: Stacie Dozier
Art Director: Nancy Sharkey
Assistant Art Director: Armando Baéz
Production Manager: Penny Gibson
Production Editor: Nicole Cypher
Desktop Specialist: Eric Dawson
Manufacturing Supervisor: Della Smith
Marketing Manager: Marge Curson
Cover Illustration: Karen Loccisano

Printed in the United States of America
6 7 8 9 10 05 04 03 02 01 00

ISBN 0–835–90981–6

Contents

Cast of Characters

La Sorelli	The lead dancer and a kind of "big sister" to the young dancers
Jammes	A young dancer in the ballet company
Meg Giry	A young dancer in the ballet company
Mr. Moncharmin	One of the two new managers of the Opera
Mr. Richard	Moncharmin's quick-tempered partner
Christine Daaè	The singer whom the Angel of Music helps; she loves Raoul de Chagny.
Raoul de Chagny	The young nobleman who loves Christine Daaè
Philippe de Chagny	A wealthy nobleman and the older brother of Raoul
Mrs. Giry	Meg Giry's mother and the boxkeeper for the Opera Ghost's Box 5
Mrs. Valérius	A woman who has known Christine since she was a child and is like a mother to her
Carlotta	The lead singer at the Opera who becomes jealous of Christine Daaè
Mr. Mifroid	The police inspector called in to solve Christine's disappearance
The Persian	The man who helps Raoul find Christine; he was a policeman in Persia.
The Opera Ghost	The man around whom the Opera mystery revolves

Prologue: How the Author Learned that the Opera Ghost Really Existed

The Opera Ghost was real. He was not imaginary, as many people had thought. He was a real person, but he did take the form of a phantom.

When I went through the official records, I found some amazing coincidences. The kidnapping of Christine Daaè, the disappearance of Raoul de Chagny, and the death of his brother Philippe were all connected to the ghost. No one had realized this. But I saw the truth.

I found the man called "the Persian." He had known the ghost for years. He told me what had happened at the Opera house. And he gave me proof, including letters belonging to Christine Daaè. I verified that the handwriting was hers. After checking the background of the Persian, I was convinced. The ghost was not a myth!

Finally I went to the Opera house. A dead body found there proved what the Persian had told me. But I will return to that story later.

I want to thank everyone I talked to who was involved in the events of this story. These people were all of great help to me. Thanks to them I am able to tell you this story of love and terror.

Gaston Leroux

1 The Opera Ghost

The story begins on the night the managers of the Opera were giving a performance to mark their retirement. La Sorelli, one of the major dancers, was alone in her dressing room. Suddenly her room was invaded by six young dancers. Some were laughing nervously and some were crying in fear.

"It's the ghost!" exclaimed young Jammes. And she locked the door.

La Sorelli shuddered. She believed in ghosts, especially the Opera Ghost. So she asked for details.

"Have you seen him?"

"As plainly as I see you now," moaned Jammes, as she dropped into a chair.

"If that's the ghost, he's very ugly," said little Meg Giry, another dancer.

"Oh, yes!" cried the others. They all began to talk at once. The ghost had appeared as a gentleman dressed in evening clothes. He had stood before them in the hallway. They didn't know where he had come from. He seemed to come right through the wall.

For months, the only thing discussed at the Opera had been this ghost. Dressed in evening clothes, he roamed the building from top to bottom like a shadow. The evening suit covered a skeleton. At least, that is what the ballet dancers had said. And of course, the skeleton was topped by a death's head. The idea of the skeleton and death's head had come from Joseph Buquet, the chief scene-changer for the Opera. Buquet had seen the ghost, and he had described him. "He is extremely thin, and his suit hangs on a skeleton frame. His eyes are so deep you can hardly see his pupils. You just see two dark holes, as in a dead man's skull. His skin is stretched across his bones, and it is a nasty yellow color. His nose is so little you can't see it from the side. The absence of the nose is horrible to look at. His only hair is three or four long dark strands on his forehead and behind his ears."

Joseph Buquet was a serious man, so his description was taken with interest. Some people said the scene-changer was the victim of a practical joke. But then, one after another, a string of strange accidents happened. Even the most skeptical people began to feel nervous.

One time, a fireman had gone to inspect the cellars and went a little farther than usual. He returned shaking and pale. He said he had seen a head of fire with no body attached!

Another time, Mr. Gabriel, the Chorus master, had been in the managers' office when a man known as "the Persian" came in.

Young Jammes told the story. "You know the Persian has the evil eye. . . ."

"Oh, yes!" cried the other dancers.

"And you know how superstitious Gabriel is!" continued young Jammes. "So he is always polite when he meets the Persian. But he puts his hand in his pocket to touch his keys, to touch iron. That keeps the evil spirits away, you know.

"Anyway, this one day he saw the Persian in the doorway, and he jumped up to touch the iron lock on the cupboard. When he did, he tore his coat on a nail. In his rush to get out of the room, he banged his head on a coat peg. When he stepped back, he skinned his arm on a screen near the piano. He tried to catch his balance on the piano, but the lid fell down and crushed his fingers. He ran out of the office like a madman. Then he slipped and fell down a whole flight of stairs.

"I was passing by with Mother. We picked him up. He was covered with bruises and his face was all bloody. We were frightened half to death. But Gabriel thanked the Lord for having escaped so easily. He said that behind the Persian he had seen the ghost. It had a death's head, just as Joseph Buquet had said!"

After her story, there was a silence. Little Meg Giry broke it. "Joseph Buquet should keep quiet. That's what Mother thinks, anyway."

"And why does your mother think that?" asked another dancer.

"Oh, I swore not to tell!" gasped Meg.

The dancers begged her to tell and promised to keep the secret. Finally she explained about the private seats in Box 5. She said that the seats there belonged only to the ghost. No one else was supposed to use them. And the seats in Box 5 were never sold.

"And does the ghost really come there?" asked someone.

"Yes," said Meg.

"Then someone must have seen him there!"

"That's just it!" continued Meg. "The ghost is not seen. Evening clothes, and all that talk about a death's head or a head on fire! That's nonsense! Mother has never seen him, but she has heard him. Mother knows he's there, because she leaves him a program. But. . . I should have held my tongue. If Mother finds out I've told you. . . . Anyway, Joseph Buquet had no business saying those things about the ghost. It will bring him bad luck. Mother said so last night."

Suddenly there was a sound of heavy feet in the hallway, and a voice called out. Young

Jammes opened the door. Her mother burst into the room and dropped into a vacant chair. Her eyes rolled back and forth madly.

"Joseph Buquet is dead!" she moaned.

The room exploded with cries of disbelief.

"He was found hanging in the third-floor cellar, below the theater," Jammes' mother explained.

"It's the ghost!" Meg Giry blurted out. But right away she covered her mouth. "I didn't say that."

The truth is that no one ever found out how Joseph Buquet died. The coroner called it a "natural death." But it seemed very unnatural. First someone found the man hanging from a rope. But when he came back to cut Buquet down, the rope was gone.

The news spread quickly. Everyone left their dressing rooms and headed for the foyer.

In the foyer the farewell ceremony for the retiring managers was underway. Speeches were being given, and the two men were smiling and cheerful.

Suddenly young Jammes broke the happiness with an exclamation: "The Opera Ghost!" There was terror in her voice and her finger pointed at a face. It was pale and ugly, with two deep black holes for eyes.

Everyone tried to laugh, and some even offered the ghost a drink. But he slipped through the crowd and was gone. People tried to calm young Jammes and also Meg Giry, who was screaming at the top of her lungs.

The two new managers, Mr. Moncharmin and Mr. Richard, had received the keys to the Opera doors. These were being passed around until someone noticed a figure seated at the end of the table. It was the same strange face with the hollow eyes that had caused young Jammes to shout.

There he sat as natural as can be, except that he neither ate nor drank. The two retiring managers got more and more nervous. They took the new managers off to the privacy of the office. There, they took out a copy of the Opera lease. It described the duties of the manager. But at the end there were two items written in red ink:

1. The manager shall pay the Opera Ghost 20,000 francs a month.

2. Box 5 shall be reserved for the Opera Ghost for every performance.

The new managers thought this was a joke. They laughed and stood up to shake hands with the two retiring managers.

Mr. Richard said chuckling, "If I had such a troublesome ghost as this one, I would have him arrested. . . ."

"But how? When?" the retiring managers answered in chorus.

"When he comes to the box," suggested Mr. Richard.

"But we have never seen him in his box!"

"Then sell the seats in the box." said Mr. Richard and Mr. Moncharmin.

With that, all four managers left the office. Mr. Richard and Mr. Moncharmin never laughed so much in their lives.

2 The Voice

The managers all went back to the foyer, which was now filled with people. Everyone was talking about the evening's performance. It had been a triumph. All the great composers had conducted their works. And the young singer Christine Daaè had sung brilliantly from *Romeo and Juliet* and from *Faust*. She had performed in place of Carlotta, who was ill, and her voice was excellent. No one had ever heard anything like it.

But some in the audience were puzzled. Why had this great talent been kept from them? Did the managers know about her voice? Meg Giry claimed that Christine Daaè couldn't sing a note six months ago. The whole thing was a mystery.

Standing in his box, the Count Philippe de Chagny had applauded wildly. With him was his younger brother Raoul, whom he had helped raise after their father's death. Raoul had just been chosen as a member of an Arctic Circle expedition. He now was on a six-month leave before going to the North Pole. Raoul was very shy. At 21, he looked about 18. But tonight, in spite of his shyness, he repeatedly asked his older brother to take him backstage. He wanted to speak to Christine Daaè.

Now standing in the foyer, Philippe looked at his brother and saw that he was very pale.

"I just heard someone say that Christine has fainted," said Raoul. "We must go and see."

Raoul led the way through the crowd. They made their way to Christine, who had still not awakened. The doctor had just arrived. Raoul asked everyone else to leave the room. So Christine awoke in the company of her maid, Raoul, and the doctor. When she saw Raoul, she was startled. She smiled at the doctor and at her maid. Then she looked at Raoul.

"Who are you, sir?" she whispered.

"I am the little boy who long ago went into the sea to rescue your scarf," replied Raoul, kissing her hand. Christine started to laugh.

"Christine," replied Raoul, very embarrassed, "don't you recognize me? I would like to speak to you alone. It is very important."

Suddenly Christine stood up and announced, "I am not ill any more. Thank you. Please, all of you, go away. I would like to be alone. I feel very restless this evening."

Raoul found himself in the hallway outside Christine's dressing room. It was deserted now, since the farewell ceremony was going on in the foyer. He hid in the shadow of a doorway, hoping

Christine would come out. He had a terrible pain in his heart. It was this he wanted to talk to her about.

Hardly breathing, Raoul approached the door and started to knock. But his hand dropped. He heard a man's voice saying, "Christine, do you love me? You must love me!"

Christine's voice, sad and trembling, replied, "How can you talk like that? I sing only for you!"

Raoul's heart pounded like thunder. If the loud pounding continued, he knew they would hear it inside the room.

The man spoke again. "Are you very tired?"

"Oh, tonight I gave you my soul, and now I am dead!" Christine replied.

"Your soul is a beautiful thing," said the man's voice, "and I thank you. No one ever received such a gift. You sang like an angel."

Raoul heard nothing further. He went around the corner, determined to wait until the man left. He loved Christine and hated the man, whoever he was. He wanted to see this person he hated. Suddenly the door opened, and Christine came out alone. She passed Raoul without noticing him. He did not follow her. His eyes were fixed on the door.

He crossed the hallway, opened the door, and went in. He stood in total darkness.

"I know you're here," said Raoul. "Where are you hiding?"

Only silence and darkness answered. He struck a match. There was no one in the room. He looked everywhere. Nothing.

"I must be going mad," he said to himself.

Raoul left the room and walked around the Opera house. He found himself at a door at the bottom of a staircase. Down came a group of workers carrying a stretcher covered with a sheet.

"Please let us by," said one of the men.

Raoul pointed to the stretcher and asked, "Who is that?"

"That is Joseph Buquet, who was found below, in the third cellar. He was hanging by his neck amid the scenery."

Raoul removed his hat and stepped out of the way. Then he went out the door.

3 The Mystery in Box 5

Mr. Richard and Mr. Moncharmin, the two new managers, were busy enjoying their first days at the Opera. They were so busy, in fact, that they forgot all about the ghost.

When Mr. Richard got to his office, his secretary gave him several unopened letters marked "private." One of them caught Mr. Richard's eye. It was written in red ink, and the handwriting looked familiar. It was the same clumsy writing as on the Opera lease.

Dear Mr. Manager:

I am sorry to trouble you when you must be very busy. However I am happy that you haven't turned Christine Daaè out onto the streets. I ask you to hear her sing tonight. She will perform the role of Siebel in Faust.

Also, I must ask you not to sell my box seats today or any other day. I cannot tell you how disappointed I have been to find my seats sold at your orders.

I know you are aware of my additions to the Opera lease. So I am warning you: If you wish to live in peace, do not take away my private box.

Your most obedient and humble servant,
Opera Ghost

Mr. Richard had just finished reading when his partner entered with an identical package.

"It's the retired managers," said Mr. Richard. "They are keeping up the joke. But I don't think it's funny any more."

"What do you think they want?" asked Mr. Moncharmin. "The seats in Box 5 for tonight?"

Mr. Richard asked his secretary to send the tickets off right away to the retired managers. The new managers were surprised that two elderly men would be playing such childish tricks. But they shrugged their shoulders and said that the men seemed very interested in young Christine Daaè.

The next morning the managers each received a card of thanks:

Dear Mr. Manager:
Thanks. Charming evening. Daaè was excellent. Carlotta was average. Will write soon for my money.
Kind regards,
Opera Ghost

There was also a letter from the two retired managers:

Gentlemen:
We are grateful for your offer of the tickets. However, we cannot use Box 5. It belongs exclusively to him. See Clause 98, final paragraph, in the lease.
Sincerely,
Mr. Poligny and Mr. Debienne,
Former Opera Managers

"Those two are beginning to annoy me!" shouted Mr. Richard.

That evening the seats in Box 5 were sold again. The next morning, the managers received a report. It was written by an Opera security inspector who had been called to Box 5 the night before.

It was necessary to call the police twice this evening to clear Box 5. The occupants of the box bothered the audience with their laughter and comments. The whole house complained. I entered the box and spoke to the occupants. They did not seem to be in their right minds and they made stupid remarks. Twice after that they continued to make noise. Finally I returned with the municipal officer, who made them leave.

"Call the inspector!" shouted Mr. Richard. The managers' secretary did so, and the inspector arrived immediately.

"Tell us what happened," said Mr. Richard.

"They must have been drinking, sir. They seemed more interested in fooling around than in listening to the music. As soon as they entered the box, they came out again and asked if the box was already occupied. They said they had heard a voice say that the box was taken!"

"But there was no one in the box, was there?" roared Mr. Richard.

"Not a soul, sir! And not in the box on the right nor in the box on the left! Not a soul, I swear!"

"And what did the boxkeeper say?"

"Oh, she said it was just the Opera Ghost," the inspector said and grinned. But he soon saw that was a mistake. Mr. Richard became furious.

"Send for the boxkeeper!" he shouted. "Bring her to me this minute!"

The boxkeeper soon arrived and introduced herself. "You know me. I'm Mrs. Giry. The mother of Meg Giry, the dancer," she said in a proud and serious voice.

Mr. Richard was impressed by her tone. But then he looked at her faded dress and worn shoes.

"Never heard of her!" he declared. "Just tell us what happened last night!"

Mrs. Giry turned red at his rudeness. Then she said in a confident voice, "I'll tell you what happened. The ghost has been annoyed again!"

Seeing that Mr. Richard was about to lose his temper completely, Mr. Moncharmin took over the questioning. Mrs. Giry was not surprised at what had happened. She considered it normal for a voice to say the box was taken. She could only explain that the voice was the ghost. She said she had often heard him speak.

"And have you spoken to this ghost, Madame?" asked Mr. Moncharmin.

"Yes! As clearly as I am now speaking to you, sir!"

"What does he say when he speaks to you?"

"Well, he once told me to bring him a footstool."

Mr. Richard burst out laughing, as did Mr. Moncharmin and the secretary. Only the inspector did not laugh.

"A ghost asking for a footstool! Then this ghost of yours is a woman?" suggested Mr. Moncharmin.

"No, the ghost is a man."

"How do you know?"

"He has a man's voice," Mrs. Giry explained. "The first time I heard him I looked in the box. But I saw nobody! Then I heard a voice say, 'Don't be frightened, Madame. I am the Opera Ghost!' The voice was so soft and kind I hardly felt frightened. And the voice came from the corner chair, on the right, in the front row.

"At the end of each performance, he gives me two francs. Sometimes he gives me five, even ten when he hasn't come to a performance for many days. But since people are annoying him lately, he gives me nothing at all."

"And how does he give you the money?"

"He leaves it on a little shelf in the box. Sometimes I find flowers, too. One day I found a rose that must have dropped off his lady's dress. Another day he left a fan behind. I brought it back to the box the next night. He took it back, and in its place he left me my favorite English candy."

"That will do, Mrs. Giry. You can go." When she had gone, the managers told the inspector they had decided to fire the madwoman. And when the inspector left, they told the secretary to prepare his final pay, too.

Left alone, the two managers decided to look into the matter of Box 5 themselves. They walked down into the theater and looked at the box. The stage hands had gone for a break, and the two men were alone in the huge, gloomy theater.

Perhaps the emptiness of the theater affected them. Maybe the darkness caused a kind of hallucination. At any rate, both Richard and Moncharmin saw a shape in the box. Neither of them said anything. Their eyes stayed fixed on

the spot, but the shape disappeared. They went out into the lobby to compare impressions. They were not at all alike. Moncharmin had seen something that looked like a death's head on the ledge. Richard had seen an old woman who looked like Mrs. Giry. Laughing like madmen, the two men ran to Box 5 again. This time they saw no shape of any kind.

They searched the box for the figure. They moved the chairs and felt around on the carpet. They went down to the box below. But they found nothing worth mentioning.

"Someone is making a fool of us," Mr. Richard said. "On Saturday there will be a performance of *Faust*. We'll watch it from Box 5 ourselves."

4 The Enchanted Violin

After her triumphant night, Christine Daaè sang only once more. She then refused requests to perform. It was as if she was afraid to sing again.

Raoul tried to see her. He wrote to her at the Opera and got no response. Finally one day he received a note.

Sir:
I do remember the little boy who went into the sea to rescue my scarf. I am going to Perros to fulfill a duty. Tomorrow is the anniversary of my father's death. You knew him, and he was very fond of you. He is buried at Perros, with his violin, in the graveyard of the little church. It is at the bottom of the hill where we played as children and where, when we were older, we said goodbye.
Christine

Raoul checked the railroad schedule and packed a small bag. He wrote a note to his brother and took a cab to the station. He spent the train ride thinking about Christine's letter. He recalled memories of their childhood.

Christine's father had been a great violinist. Her mother had died when she was six, so her father raised her. He wandered through the countryside with his daughter, playing his violin. Christine would sing to his music. A man named Professor Valérius heard them and took them home with him. The professor provided Christine's education, and Mrs. Valérius became like a mother to her.

When Professor and Mrs. Valérius went to Paris, the Daaès also went. But Mr. Daaè was homesick for the sea, so the whole family went to Perros, on the coast. There he was happier.

One day a little boy and his governess walked on the beach near Christine and her father. The boy heard Christine singing and he became interested in her. A high wind took her scarf out to sea. She gave a cry, then heard a voice say, "It's all right. I'll go and get it out of the sea."

After that day Mr. Daaè gave Raoul music lessons, and the two young people played together. They would go door to door asking people to tell them stories. Most everyone had a story to tell. A special treat was when Christine's father would tell about the Angel of Music. Sometimes the Angel would lean over a baby's crib, and the child would become a musical genius. Other times the Angel would not come because the children were naughty and wouldn't practice their lessons. No one ever saw the Angel, but he was heard by those who were meant to hear him.

When Christine asked if he had heard the Angel, her father shook his head sadly. But he said, "One day you will, my child! When I am in Heaven, I'll send him to you!"

When Raoul saw Christine many years later at the Opera, he was surprised at her singing. It was indifferent, without emotion. He went often to the theater to hear her. He followed her backstage and tried to get her attention. But she never seemed to notice him. Then came the triumphant evening when she sang at the gala performance. That night she sang like an angel, and her angelic voice captured his heart.

But then she didn't seem to know him. She had even laughed at him. And there was the man's voice: "You must love me." So why had she written to him now?

Arriving at Perros, Raoul found Christine at the inn, the Setting Sun. She was not surprised to see him.

"So you have come. My father, who is dead, told me you were here."

"Did your father also tell you that I love you, Christine? And that I cannot live without you?"

"I did not ask you to come here to tell me such things. I thought you would remember our childhood games. I really don't know what I thought. Perhaps I was wrong to write to you. . . ."

There was something unnatural about Christine. There was sadness and tenderness in her eyes. Raoul began to feel confused.

"You did recognize me in your dressing room. Why did you pretend not to know me? Why did you laugh at me?"

Raoul's manner was so rough that Christine was surprised. He continued, "You don't answer! I'll answer for you. I heard someone in your room. Someone to whom you said, 'I sing only for you! . . . Tonight I gave you my soul!' "

At those words, Christine's face became deathly pale. Her eyes went blank. Raoul was afraid. Suddenly her eyes moistened, and two giant tears ran down her cheeks. Raoul tried to take her in his arms, but she ran away.

All the next day, Raoul did not see Christine. He walked to the church to look for her. The church was constructed in a strange way. Hundreds of skeletons and skulls were piled against the outside wall. These were held in place by wire that left the awful pile visible. Other bones were arranged in rows to make up the actual foundation of the church. The door to the altar opened in the middle of the bony structure.

Raoul went in and said a prayer for Mr. Daaè. Then he climbed the hill and sat looking at the sea. As night fell, he heard Christine's voice behind him.

"I have decided to tell you something important," she said. "Do you remember the story of the Angel of Music?"

"Of course," Raoul answered. "It was here that your father first told it to us."

"And he said, 'When I am in Heaven, my child, I will send him to you.' Well, Raoul, my father is in Heaven. And I have been visited by the Angel of Music."

"I have no doubt of that, Christine. No human can sing the way you sang the other evening. It had to be a miracle. I believe you have heard the Angel of Music."

"You do understand?" she asked with surprise. "He comes to give me lessons every day—in my dressing room."

"In your dressing room?" Raoul echoed.

"Yes, that is what you heard, my friend. It was the Angel of Music who was talking when you were listening at the door. It was he who said, 'You must love me.' But I thought I was the only one who could hear his voice. Imagine how surprised I was when you told me you heard him, too."

Raoul burst out laughing. Christine turned to him with a cold look.

"Why are you laughing? You don't believe me? You think you heard a man, I suppose. I am an honest girl, and I don't lock myself up with men. If you had opened the door, you would have seen there was no one there."

"That's true! I did open the door, and there was no one."

"So you see, then?"

"Christine, someone is playing a joke on you."

At that, Christine gave a cry and ran away. Back at the inn she did not come down for dinner. Raoul waited as the hours passed. Just before midnight he heard Christine's door open and then the innkeeper's voice saying: "Don't lose the key."

Raoul looked out and saw Christine's white form below. He climbed out the window and down a tree growing against the wall. He followed Christine, not making any attempt to be quiet. He wanted her to see him, but she didn't. She went to the churchyard, knelt beside her father's grave, and prayed. Soon the clock struck midnight. At the last stroke Christine raised her arms toward the sky in joy.

Suddenly there was the most perfect music. It sounded like Mr. Daaé's violin. If the Angel of Music existed, he could not have played more perfectly. When the music stopped, Raoul heard a noise from behind the heap of skulls. It was as

if someone was chuckling. Thinking perhaps a musician was hiding there, Raoul went to look. For that reason he didn't follow Christine when she left the churchyard.

As Raoul approached the wall of the church, skulls began to roll at his feet. He saw a shadow glide across the wall. He caught the corner of a coat and did not let go. The shadow turned and faced Raoul. A death's head stared at him with scorching eyes. Raoul's heart gave way, and he fainted.

The next morning Raoul was carried back to the inn. He had been found unconscious, stretched full length on the altar inside the little church.

5 The Fatal Performance

Saturday morning the Opera managers received a letter written in red ink.

My Dear Managers:
So it is to be war between us?
If you still want peace, here are my four conditions:
1. Give back my private box. It must be reserved only for me from now on.
2. Have Christine Daaè sing the part of Marguerite tonight. Don't worry about Carlotta. She will be ill.
3. Rehire my loyal boxkeeper, Mrs. Giry, right away.
4. Agree to pay my monthly allowance. Give a note about this to Mrs. Giry. She will see that it gets to me.
If you refuse these conditions, Faust will be performed tonight in a theater with a curse on it. Take my advice and be warned in time.
O.G.

"I'm getting sick of his threats!" shouted Mr. Richard, banging his fists on his desk.

Just then the stable manager of the Opera came to see the managers. The Opera had 12 horses kept in a stable in the cellars of the theater. The horses were trained to be used in the performances.

"Eleven horses," said the stable manager. "I did have 12, but there are only 11 now. César was stolen. I don't know how."

"César, the white horse? You must have some idea how!" exclaimed Mr. Richard.

"Well, yes, I have," the stable manager declared. "I'll tell you what I think. There's no doubt in my mind." He walked closer to the managers and whispered, "It's the ghost."

Mr. Richard jumped up and shouted. "You can go now. I've heard enough!"

As the stable manager left, Mrs. Giry entered. She held a letter in her hand.

"I'm sorry to bother you, but I have this letter from the Opera Ghost. He says that you have something . . ."

The poor woman never finished her sentence. Mr. Richard gave her a very rude exit out the door.

Just about the same time, Carlotta was brought some letters as she was having breakfast in bed. Among them was one in red ink and clumsy handwriting:

If you appear tonight, be prepared for a misfortune. When you open your mouth to sing, a terrible thing will happen.

Carlotta lost her appetite for breakfast. She was sure Christine Daaè was behind this. Carlotta always thought there was a plot against her. She was furious about the good reviews Christine had received, and she had put a stop to them. So Carlotta thought for a while and came up with an idea. She called all her friends and asked them to come to the theater that night to applaud for her.

Mr. Richard called from the Opera to ask about her health. Carlotta said she was well and that, even if she were dying, she would sing the part of Marguerite that night.

At five o'clock, a second anonymous letter arrived. It said simply:

You have a bad cold. If you are wise, do not try to sing tonight.

Carlotta sang a few notes to reassure herself she was healthy.

That evening, Carlotta's friends packed the house. The stage was set for the performance of *Faust*. The two managers took their places in Box 5, and the curtain rose for the first act.

That act ended without incident. As the two managers left the box for a short time during the intermission, Mr. Richard remarked to his partner, "The ghost is late."

The second act began. The dancers leaped and whirled. Christine Daaè made her entrance as Siebel. Carlotta's friends expected something to happen, but it did not.

Between the second and third acts the managers again left the box. When they returned, the first thing they saw was a box of English candy on the ledge shelf. They asked who put it there, but no one knew. Then they saw a pair of opera glasses next to the candy. They looked at one another. Everything Mrs. Giry had told them came to mind. Then they felt a strong draft. They sat down in silence.

The next scene opened with Christine as Siebel. As she sang her lines, she saw Raoul in his box. At the sight of him her voice became less sure and clear. Her singing had lost its life.

Raoul put his head in his hands and wept. He thought about the letter he had received when he got back from Perros:

My Dear Little Playmate:
You must have the courage not to see me again. And you must not speak of me either. If you love me, do this for me. Your life depends on it. I will never forget you, dear Raoul.
Your Christine

Carlotta made her entrance as Marguerite. Her friends applauded loudly. She felt very sure of herself. It seemed that Carlotta was about to have a new success.

Faust, kneeling, sang of his love:
"Let me gaze on the form below me. . .
To love thy beauty too!"
And Marguerite replied:
"Oh, how strange!
Like a spell does the evening bind me! . . ."
At that moment, a terrible thing happened. Carlotta croaked like a frog: "Co-ack!"

Everyone was horrified, including Carlotta. She tried to convince herself that it had not happened.

Meanwhile in Box 5, the managers were filled with dread. They had come under the spell of the ghost. Mr. Moncharmin's hair stood on end. Mr. Richard perspired. The ghost was all around them, beside them, behind them. They felt his presence without seeing him. They heard his breath close, closer. They thought of running away, but they didn't dare to move. What was going to happen? And then they heard: "Co-ack!"

Mr. Richard's stifled voice called for Carlotta to go on. Her voice again filled the house:
"I feel without alarm — co-ack!
With its melody unwind me —co-ack!
With all my heart — co-ack!"

The house was in an uproar. The managers sank in their chairs. The ghost was laughing behind them. They clearly heard his voice: "She sings tonight to bring down the chandelier!"

At once, the two managers raised their eyes. The huge chandelier on the ceiling was slipping down. It came toward them at the call of the ghost's voice. Its hook released, and it plunged to the ground. There were a thousand shouts of terror. People rushed wildly for the doors.

The newspapers reported that many people were injured and one killed. The victim was a poor woman who had come to the Opera for the first time in her life. It was said she was a guest of Mr. Richard, and that she had come with her husband and son. She died instantly.

6 The Red Death

The evening was tragic for everyone. Carlotta became ill. Christine disappeared. A month passed without her being seen. Raoul tried to find her. He wrote to her at the Valérius's address but got no reply. The Opera managers acted as if they were overcome by some terrible thought.

The police investigation ended with a verdict of accidental death. The report said the accident was caused by wear and tear on the chains from which the chandelier hung.

Mrs. Giry had been rehired in her previous job. When Raoul inquired at the Opera about Christine, Mrs. Giry told him that Christine had left for health reasons.

Raoul decided to go see Mrs. Valérius.

"Madame, where is Christine?" he asked at once.

The old lady replied calmly, "She is with her Angel of Music! But you must not tell anyone." She put her finger to her lips. "Poor, Raoul. I am very fond of you. And Christine is, too! But you know she is not free. She cannot marry, even if she wanted to."

"I don't know anything about that! Why can't Christine marry?"

"Because of the Angel of Music, of course. He forbids her to marry—without telling her as much. He tells her that she will never hear him again if she is married. That's all. And you understand she cannot let the Angel of Music go. I thought Christine told you all this when she met you at Perros. She went there with her Angel."

"She went to Perros with her Angel of Music, did she?" asked Raoul.

"He arranged to meet her there, at her father's grave. He promised to play her father's violin."

"Now I see! I see!" Raoul cried and rushed out. When he got home, he collapsed. His brother asked for no explanation. But he told Raoul that Christine had been seen in the Boulogne Park. She had been riding in a carriage with a man. As for the man, he was described only as a shadowy outline leaning back in the dark.

That night Raoul went to the park at ten o'clock. After waiting a while, he saw a carriage turn the corner. It came toward him very slowly. As it approached, he saw a woman leaning her head out the window.

"Christine!" he shouted without meaning to. Immediately, he wished he had not.

The window closed and the carriage rushed past him. His heart turned cold. She did not love him! What would he do? He saw no future for himself, and he was only 21 years old! Raoul went home an extremely sad young man.

In the morning a letter came. Raoul recognized the handwriting. The note read:

My Dear:
Go to the masked ball at the Opera the night after tomorrow. At midnight stand near the door to the foyer. Don't mention this to anyone on earth. Wear a white costume. As you love me, do not let anyone recognize you.
Christine

The envelope was muddy and unstamped. It looked as if it had been thrown out of a window in the hope someone would pick it up.

Raoul's thoughts flew back and forth. Was she a helpless victim, an innocent young woman? Did she really love him after all?

Then Raoul remembered the Angel of Music. Now this Angel was taking her for rides in the park. What games was she playing with him? Raoul didn't know what to think. But he bought a white costume for the ball.

Just before midnight, he climbed the stairs to the Opera foyer. He waited near the door, but not for long. Someone in a black costume touched his fingers. He understood it was

Christine, and he followed her. He was ready to forgive her. He knew she could explain her actions. He was in love.

As he followed Christine, Raoul noticed a group crowding around someone. It was a man dressed all in red, with a huge hat and feathers on top of a death's head. He wore a large red velvet cloak embroidered with the words, "Don't touch me. I am the Red Death!"

Passing this person, Raoul nearly spoke aloud. He had recognized the figure and wanted to shout, "The Death's Head of Perros!"

He stopped, but the black costume pulled him along. They went up two floors and into a private box. Christine put her ear against the door. Then she opened it and looked into the corridor.

"He must have gone higher," she said. Then suddenly, she added, "He's coming down again."

Raoul held the door open. He saw a red foot, followed by another. Slowly the entire robe of the Red Death met his eyes. He saw again the death's head he had seen in the graveyard at Perros. He was about to rush out to confront the figure, but Christine held him back.

Raoul cried, "It's the evil thing from the churchyard! The Red Death! He is your friend, your Angel of Music! I want to see him. There will be no more lies between us! I must see the man you love!"

Christine flung out her arms against the door. "In the name of our love, Raoul, do not pass!"

"You lie. You don't love me. You never loved me! You've deceived me! I hate you. . . ."

"One day, Raoul, you will beg my forgiveness for those ugly words. And, when you do, I will forgive you."

With those words, Christine walked away.

"Christine, please come back!" Raoul called. He watched her until she was out of sight. Then he wandered aimlessly. He found himself outside her dressing room. He had just gone inside the room when he heard footsteps. He only had time to hide behind the curtain. Christine entered.

She sighed and let her head fall into her hands. He heard her murmur, "Poor Erik!"

Then there was singing. The song became clearer and stronger. It was inside the room.

Christine stood and said to the voice, "Here I am, Erik. I'm ready. But you are late." The voice sang on. Raoul had never heard anything so beautiful, so powerful. Now he understood how Christine had sung so well under its influence.

Christine walked toward her own image in the mirror. As she met it, she disappeared. Worn out and beaten, Raoul fell into a chair. Like Christine, he held his head in his hands and wondered aloud, "Who is this Erik?"

The next day Raoul went to see Mrs. Valérius again. He was astonished to find Christine there.

She stood and, showing no emotion, shook the hand Raoul offered formally.

"Mr. de Chagny," said Mrs. Valérius, "why so formal? You know our Christine. Her Angel has sent her back to us."

"Mama!" Christine broke in. "I have vowed to explain everything to you one day. But you have promised me, until that day, to ask no more questions!"

Raoul turned pale. He had caught sight of a plain gold ring on Christine's finger.

"What is this? A wedding ring?" he demanded as he tried to take her hand.

"It is a present," Christine said, drawing back swiftly.

"Christine, that ring is a promise offered and accepted. You are under a dangerous spell. I have heard the voice. Please, Christine, tell me the name of the man who put that ring on your finger!"

"Mr. de Chagny," the young woman said coldly, "you will never know."

"Christine, I know. It is Erik. The name of your Angel of Music is Erik!"

"Oh, you poor man," moaned Christine. She seemed terrified. "Do you want to die? Forget the man's voice and forget his name! Promise me you will never try to understand the mystery! And swear that you will never come to my dressing room again unless I send for you."

"But will you send for me, Christine?"

"Yes, I will. Tomorrow."

"Then today I will do as you ask," said Raoul in a sad voice.

He went away, cursing Erik but determined to be patient.

7 Above the Trapdoors

The next day Raoul saw Christine at the Opera. She was still wearing the gold ring, but she was much kinder to him.

He reminded her that he would be leaving soon for the North Pole. The Polar expedition would start in one month. Suddenly Christine seemed to be thinking up a new idea. Her eyes glowed with it.

She gave Raoul both her hands. "Raoul, I am thinking that in a month we shall have to say goodbye forever. And that we shall never be married. That is understood. But if we can't be married, we can. . . we can be engaged! Nobody needs to know but us. We can be engaged for a month!"

Raoul jumped at the idea. "Christine, I have the honor to ask for your hand in marriage."

"You already have them both, my dear! We will be very happy!"

It was a game, and they enjoyed it as they had enjoyed their childhood games. But one day, about a week after the game began, Raoul's heart was sad. He uttered these words: "I'm not going to leave you! I won't go to the North Pole!"

Christine had never dreamed this would happen. She saw how dangerous their game was. She said nothing and went straight home.

For two days Christine stayed away. But when she returned to the Opera, she came in triumph. She sang as she had for the gala performance, and she received thunderous applause. Afterwards, Raoul ran backstage.

He threw himself to his knees. He swore he would go on the expedition as they had planned. He begged her not to stay away from him again.

Over the next weeks, Raoul and Christine explored the Opera house together. One day Raoul sat on the set while Christine practiced. Another day the two wandered through the gardens. Then Christine took Raoul above the stage, to the wardrobe and prop rooms. The Opera house—her castle—was 17 stories high. And she walked through it like a queen.

Days passed with these adventures. Then Christine began to get nervous. Sometimes her eyes followed imaginary shadows. Once, when she and Raoul walked over an open trapdoor on the stage, Raoul made a request.

"I have seen the upper part of your castle, Christine. But there are tales told of the lower part. Let's go down through the trapdoor. I want to see beneath the stage. Will you show me that?"

"Never! I will not let you go down there! Besides, that part of the Opera is not mine. Everything that is underground belongs to him." She dragged Raoul away. Suddenly the trapdoor closed shut with a bang. Neither spoke for a moment.

"Perhaps he was down there listening. He may have heard us talking," Raoul said at last.

"No, no. I know he has shut himself up. He is working."

All the same, for the next few days, the two were careful to avoid the trapdoors. But Christine grew more and more nervous.

Raoul said to her, "I will remove you from his power, Christine. I swear I will."

"Is it possible?" She asked this as she led Raoul up to the top floor of the Opera house. She needed to get far away from the trapdoors below.

"I'll hide you in some unknown corner of the world. You'll be safe there."

"Higher!" was all Christine said. "Higher still!"

Both failed to see the shadow that followed them. It stopped when they stopped. It started when they did. It made no noise.

They reached the roof. All of Paris was below them. The shadow had followed them, clinging to their steps. They did not suspect its presence.

Christine said, "Raoul, make me a promise. It is about when you will take me away. If I refuse to go, you must carry me away by force."

"Are you afraid you might change your mind?"

"I don't know," she said, shaking her head. "I know that if I don't go back to him, terrible things may happen. We only have one day left. If I don't go back, he will come for me. He'll carry me away to his house on the lake. He will tell me he loves me. He will weep those terrible tears. I can't bear to see those tears again!"

Raoul tried to drag her away, then and there. But she stopped him saying, "No, no. Let him hear me sing tomorrow evening. Then we'll go away."

"Tell me how you saw him the first time."

"I heard him for three months before I saw him. At first the voice just sang. Then it spoke to me and answered my questions. I had not yet received the Angel of Music my father had promised to send me. So I asked the voice, and it said yes, it was the Angel I was expecting. From that time on, the voice and I became good friends. It offered to give me lessons every day.

"When the voice learned about you, it became sad." Christine continued. "It told me that I must not give my heart here on earth. If I did, there would be nothing for the voice to do but go back to Heaven. I remembered my poor childhood and your high position in society. I knew we could never marry. So I told the voice you were like a brother to me. But the voice was not fooled. It became jealous of you. I told it I was going to ask you to come to Perros with me. 'Do as you please,' the voice said. 'But I will be at Perros, too. And if you have not lied to me, I will play something incredible for you on your father's violin. Be in the churchyard, at your father's grave, at midnight.'

"Oh, Raoul, how did I let myself become so deceived? I had come so far under his control!"

"But you did learn the truth finally!" said Raoul.

"Do you remember the night the chandelier fell?" Christine asked. "I was worried about you. I went to my dressing room to look for you. Then a strange thing happened. The room seemed to get longer, and I found myself outside the room in a dark hallway. I was frightened and I called out to the voice.

"Suddenly a hand, stone-cold and bony, grabbed my wrist. It did not let go. I struggled toward a small light. I could see that I was held by a man wearing a large cloak and a mask that covered his whole face. I tried to scream but his hand closed over my mouth. The hand smelled of death. Then I fainted.

"When I awoke I was still in darkness, but from the small light I could see a bubbling well. I knew I was in the first cellar under the stage of the theater. I was lying on the ground and my head was resting on the knee of the masked man. He was bathing my head with water from the well. I pushed his hand away and asked, 'Where am I? Where is the voice?' The man just sighed.

"Then he lifted me up onto a white horse. I knew it was César, the horse that had disappeared from the theater. There had been a rumor that the Opera Ghost had stolen the horse.

"I believed in the voice, but I had never believed in the ghost. Now I began to wonder if they were one and the same. I called out for the voice to help me. You have heard about the Opera Ghost, haven't you, Raoul?"

"Yes, of course. But, Christine, tell me what happened when you were on the white horse."

"I just let myself go. The masked figure held me up and a calm came over me. César went along on his own. We went down and further down, into the heart of the earth. We must have descended into the lowest cellar of the Opera. Finally, César sniffed the air and stopped. We were at the edge of a lake, and I saw a boat tied to the wharf.

"When the man lifted me into the boat, my terror began again. He sent César back, and he jumped into the boat. He rowed with quick, powerful strokes and never took his eyes off me.

"When we touched shore, he lifted me up again. I cried out, but I was silenced by a dazzling light. Suddenly I was in a sitting room decorated with many flowers. In the middle of the room stood the masked man, his arms crossed under his black robe. 'Don't be afraid, Christine,' he said. 'You are in no danger.'

"It was the voice! I rushed at him and tried to tear off his mask. I wanted to see the face that went with the voice. He held my arms and said, 'You are in no danger so long as you do not touch the mask.'

"He sat me in a chair and knelt before me. 'Christine,' the voice said, 'I have deceived you. I am not the Angel, nor am I a ghost. I am Erik!'"

Raoul repeated the name after her and then said, "Christine, we cannot wait until tomorrow. We should leave at once."

"No. If he does not hear me sing tomorrow, it will cause him great pain. He will certainly die if I leave him. But then, we risk him killing you!"

"Does he love you that much?"

"He would commit murder for me! Think of it. He confessed all his lies. He carried me off for love! He crawled, moaned, and wept. I told him I would hate him if he did not let me go.

"He showed me his apartment. His bedroom was like that of a dead person. In the middle of the room was a canopy bed around an open coffin. It was terrible. Then I saw the keyboard of an organ. 'I compose sometimes,' he said. 'I began the music 20 years ago. When I finish it, I will take it into my coffin and never wake up again.'

"I asked him to play for me. When he did, he forgot all about me and everything else around him. It was my chance to see beneath the mask. I reached out and tore it away. Oh, horror, horror! If I live to be a hundred, I'll never forget the sight or the cry of rage and grief he uttered.

"Raoul, you have seen human skulls dried and withered with age. And you have seen the mask of the Red Death. But imagine those two suddenly coming to life. Four black holes—the eyes, nose, and mouth—and the fury of a demon! He hissed and cursed me. 'Look! You wanted to see? See! Feast your eyes!' He dragged my hands to his face. 'Tear it off!' he screamed. And he dug my nails into his flesh. 'Know that it is a corpse that loves you and will never leave you!' He let go of me at last. And he crawled weeping to his room and closed the door.

"Now you know the tragedy. It went on for a month. I asked him to show me his face. And when he did, I did not look away. He told me about his childhood, how his mother gave him his first mask as a baby. She could never bear to look at him, and she finally gave him away.

"I felt sorry for him, so I lied. I told him if I ever shuddered again when I looked at him, it was because his music was so beautiful. I swore that if he let me go I would come back. After a month he believed me. He said he would let me go, and I promised to return. He gave me the gold ring when I left him."

"Christine, I am certain it would be better to leave at once. Why wait for tomorrow? He may have heard us," said Raoul.

"No, he is busy. He is working on his music. He is not thinking of us."

"Then I will be here at midnight tomorrow night. I'll keep my promise to take you away then, no matter what happens."

"Oh, heavens! Oh, dear! Erik, have pity on me!" A deathly pale spread over Christine's face.

"What is it?" Raoul begged.

"The ring. . . the gold ring he gave me. He said, 'I give you your freedom so long as you wear the ring. But a terrible fate will come to you if you lose it.' Raoul, . . . the ring is gone!"

8 The Disappearance

Raoul went home very upset by what Christine had told him. He cursed Erik aloud.

"Who is Erik?" asked his brother Philippe.

"He is my rival," Raoul answered.

Philippe handed his brother a newspaper. It was turned to the gossip column. "Read this," he said.

The latest news is a promise of love between Miss Christine Daaè, the opera singer, and the Viscount Raoul de Chagny. Rumor has it that Count Philippe intends to prevent his brother from taking Miss Daaè to the altar. The two brothers are said to be very close. But we wouldn't bet on brotherly love winning out over passion.

"You see, Raoul, your adventures are public. You are making us look ridiculous! The girl has filled your head with her ghost stories," said Philippe.

"I am going away with her tonight," said Raoul.

"Surely you wouldn't do anything so foolish? I know how to stop you!" said Philippe.

"Goodbye, Philippe," said Raoul as he left the room.

Raoul spent the day preparing for the trip. He selected the horses, carriage, and coachman. He packed food, luggage, and money. He chose the route. Before he knew it, it was nine o'clock.

At the Opera, they were performing *Faust* before a large audience. The newspaper article had an effect. All eyes were on Count Philippe as he sat alone in his box. The women in the audience whispered about Raoul's absence. They gave Christine a cool reception. After all, Christine was from a poor family, and Raoul was a wealthy nobleman. The women would not forgive her for aiming at such a high prize.

Christine was aware of their feelings. She sang with all her heart and soul. In the last act, when she began the song to the angels, everyone in the audience felt as if they, too, had wings.

Suddenly, in the center of the theater a man stood facing the singer. It was Raoul.

Christine, with arms outstretched, sang to him:

"Holy angel, in Heaven blessed . . .
My spirit longs with thee to rest!"

At that exact moment the stage plunged into darkness. Then the lights came back on. It happened so quickly that the audience barely had time to gasp. But there was confusion on the stage. Raoul let out a cry. Count Philippe jumped to his feet. People looked from the stage, to Raoul, to Philippe.

Carolus Fonta, who was singing the role of Faust that night, stepped onto the music conductor's platform and announced, "Ladies and gentlemen, a very strange thing has happened. Christine Daaè has disappeared. It happened before our very eyes but nobody knows how."

Raoul's first thought was Erik. He rushed onto the stage, calling "Christine! Christine!" He wandered around the theater like a madman. In her dressing room were the clothes she was to have worn at their hour of flight. Horrible thoughts filled his mind. Erik must have discovered their secret. He must have learned that Christine was not telling the truth. What terrible revenge he would take!

"Christine! Christine! Answer me! Are you alive?" Raoul screamed.

Raoul ran up the stairs four at a time. He went through the business section of the Opera and down to the stage again. Perhaps Christine had been found. He stopped a group of men and asked, "I beg your pardon, gentlemen. Could you tell me where Christine Daaè is?"

Somebody laughed and pointed to a man at the center of the group. The man had a pleasant face, curly hair, and calm blue eyes. "This is the man to whom you should put your question. Let me introduce you to Mr. Mifroid, the police commissioner."

"Ah, Raoul de Chagny! Delighted to meet you. Let's go to the managers' office and let them in on what's happened here!"

Raoul was the last of a large group to enter the managers' office. He was about to go into the room when he felt a hand on his shoulder and a whisper in his ear, "Erik's secrets concern no one but himself!"

Raoul turned. He saw the hand held to the lips of a man with dark skin and green eyes. The man wore a long coat and a wool hat. Raoul remembered seeing him once or twice backstage at the theater. He was known as "the Persian." Philippe had once said that the only thing he knew about this mysterious person was that he lived somewhere in Paris.

Just as Raoul was about to ask the reason for his comment, the Persian bowed and disappeared.

"Is Christine Daaè here?" Commissioner Mifroid asked the Opera managers.

"Christine Daaè here?" echoed Mr. Richard. "No. Why do you ask if she is here?"

"Because she has not been found anywhere else," declared the police commissioner.

"Found? Has she disappeared?" asked Mr. Moncharmin.

"During the performance."

"During the performance? Unbelievable!" cried the manager.

"Yes. As she was singing to the angels, she was carried off," explained the commissioner calmly. "I doubt, however, that it was an angel that took her away!"

Raoul, pale and trembling, offered a different opinion. "Oh, yes, Christine Daaè was carried off by an angel. I can give you his name. . . when we are alone."

The police commissioner cleared the room except for Raoul and the managers.

Raoul said, "Sir, the angel is called Erik. He lives in the Opera house, and he is the Angel of Music."

Turning to the managers, Mr. Mifroid asked, "Do you have an Angel of Music here?"

The two men shook their heads, without speaking.

"Oh," said Raoul, "but surely these men have heard of the Opera Ghost. The Opera Ghost and the Angel of Music are the same person. His name is Erik."

Mr. Richard stood up and said, "No, commissioner. We don't know any Erik, but we would like to meet him. He has caused us a great deal of difficulty!"

Commissioner Mifroid looked from Raoul to the managers and back again.

"A ghost," he said, "who carries off a singer. Mr. de Chagny, do you know this person? Have you seen him?"

"Yes, in a churchyard."

"Of course! That's where ghosts are often found."

"Sir," said Raoul, "To convince you, I must tell the strangest story you will have ever heard."

Raoul began to tell his story of Perros, the death's head, and the violin. His listeners thought he had lost his mind, but they never had a chance to say so. There was a knock on the door. A man entered and whispered in the commissioner's ear.

Commissioner Mifroid never took his eyes off Raoul. Finally he said, "You were going to carry off Miss Daaè yourself tonight, weren't you?"

"Yes, sir."

"After the performance?"

"Yes, sir," answered Raoul.

"And did you see your brother's carriage at the theater tonight?"

"No, sir," said Raoul.

"Well your brother is smarter than you. He is

the one who carried off Christine Daaè!"

"Impossible!" said Raoul.

"His carriage was seen crossing and leaving Paris, by the Brussels road."

Raoul jumped up and rushed out of the office. But he was stopped at the first corridor by a tall figure that blocked his way. He impatiently looked up. He recognized the coat and hat, and he stopped.

"It's you!" Raoul said. "You know Erik's secrets and tell me not to speak of them. Who are you, really?"

"You know who I am. I am the Persian."

9 Down into the Cellars

"Where are you going so fast, Mr. de Chagny?" asked the Persian.

"To Christine Daaè's assistance, of course."

"Then stay here, sir, because she is here!"

"With Erik?" Raoul asked.

"I was at the performance. No one in the world but Erik could have pulled off such a kidnapping! I recognize the monster's touch!"

"Sir," said Raoul, "the commissioner of police has just told me my brother Philippe carried Christine off. You tell me she is here! I don't know you, but I believe you. What can you do to help?"

"I can try to take you to her. . . and to him."

"Let's not waste any more time. I place myself entirely in your hands. Why wouldn't I? You're the only one who doesn't think I'm crazy when I mention Erik's name!"

"Silence! Do not say that name here. Say 'he' and 'him' instead. That way there will be less danger of attracting his attention."

"So you think he is near?" asked Raoul.

"It is possible, sir. Or maybe he's with his victim at the house at the lake. Or here in this wall, in the floor, in the ceiling! Let's go!"

The Persian led Raoul through a door opposite Christine Daaè's dressing room. Entering the room, the men listened. Then the Persian coughed softly.

From behind the screen, a man appeared, also wearing a hat and long coat. He bowed and took a carved wooden case from under his coat. He put it on the table, bowed again, and went to the door.

"Well done, Darius. Let no one see you leave," said the Persian, opening the case. Inside was a pair of long pistols. He handed one to Raoul. "In this fight, we will be two against one. But be prepared for anything. We shall be fighting the most terrible enemy you can imagine. You do love Christine Daaè, don't you?"

"I worship the ground she walks on. But you don't even know her. So you must hate Erik for another reason!"

"No, sir," said the Persian sadly. "I don't hate him. If I did, he would have been stopped long ago. But I will tell you more about him later."

The Persian climbed on a stool against the wall opposite the mirror. His nose to the wallpaper, he looked for something. Finally he seemed satisfied. He pressed a corner of the wallpaper.

"In half a minute," he said, "the mirror will turn on its pivot. Then we will be on his road!

Button up your shirt as high as possible. Bring your coat lapels together. Turn up the collar. We must make ourselves as invisible as possible."

"It's not moving," said Raoul impatiently as he stared at the mirror.

"Hold on! We shall do all that is humanly possible. But he may stop us at our first step. He commands these walls, doors, and trapdoors. In my country, he was known as 'the trapdoor lover.' Besides, he built this place."

Raoul was about to ask a question, but the Persian made a sign for him to be quiet.

"Look out!" he said, "and be ready to fire." He raised his own pistol opposite the glass. Suddenly the mirror turned like a revolving door. It took Raoul and the Persian with it, carrying them from the light into deep darkness.

"Keep your hand high, ready to fire!" the Persian repeated quickly.

The wall closed behind them. They stood still, without breathing. At last the Persian moved. Raoul heard him on his knees, feeling for something. He could not see the Persian, but he heard him whisper, "Follow me and do everything I do!"

Strangely, Raoul trusted the Persian completely. He knew nothing about him, but he had to reach Christine. So he got on his knees and hung from the trapdoor with both hands, just as the Persian had done.

"Now let go!"

Raoul dropped down beside the Persian. They lay flat, listening. Then the Persian made a sign to stand up. He immediately reminded Raoul to hold his hand up in front of his eyes.

"It tires my hand," said Raoul. "If I do fire, I won't be sure of my aim."

"Actually it's not a question of shooting. It's a question of holding one of your hands up at eye level. As for the pistol itself, you can put it in your pocket. This is a matter of life or death. I will explain later but, for now, do it and follow me!"

The Opera cellars were enormous, and there were five of them. Once the men were in the fifth one, the Persian drew a breath. He seemed more confident. But he never changed the position of his hand.

Suddenly something moved in front of them.

"On your stomach!" whispered the Persian. The two men lay on the floor. A fantastic face came into sight. . . a whole fiery face, not just two yellow eyes! It was the average height of a man, but with no body attached.

"Wow!" said the Persian. "I've never seen this before! He may have sent it. Take care! Hand at eye level! I know most of his tricks. . . but not this one! Run! It is safer. Hand at eye level!"

After a few seconds, they stopped running. The head of fire was closer behind them. It must have run, too. They ran again. The head of fire was gaining on them. They could see its features clearly now. The eyes were round and wide open, the nose crooked. The mouth was large, with a drooping lower lip. It was like a bright red moon. As the head approached, a scraping, scratching sound came with it.

The two men flattened themselves against the wall. They felt their hair stand on end. The wave of noise came toward them. They could feel the wave climb up their legs. They could not hold back cries of pain. They were forced to lower their hands to push back the wave. But it was filled with little legs and nails, claws and teeth.

"Don't move! Don't move! Whatever you do, don't come after me!" a voice called out. "I am the rat catcher! Let me pass by with my rats!"

The head of fire disappeared, and so did the wave of scratching, biting noise. In order not to scare the rats in front of him, the rat catcher had turned the light on himself. It had lit up his head. Now, to hurry the rats, he lit the dark space in front of him. He ran, dragging the rats with him.

Raoul turned to the Persian and shouted, "Take me to Christine. I must save her from this horror!"

The Persian tried to calm Raoul. "We only have one way of saving Christine. That is to enter the house without Erik seeing us. We need to go back up to the third cellar. I know the exact place. It is where Joseph Buquet died. Follow me now. Keep your hand at eye level!"

Once in the third cellar, he motioned Raoul to crawl. They came to a place where a stone gave way. The Persian motioned Raoul to follow him. Cocking their pistols, they wiggled into the hole.

The two men dropped down. The darkness was thick around them. The Persian turned on the lantern. He bent to examine something on the floor. He threw it away with horror and mumbled, "The Punjab lasso!"

"What is that?" asked Raoul.

The Persian shivered. "It might be the rope by which Joseph Buquet was hanged."

As the Persian moved the lantern, a tree trunk appeared. It looked alive. Leaves and branches ran up the walls. The light of the lantern was reflected.

Raoul said, "The wall is a mirror."

"Yes," the Persian said. "We have dropped into the torture chamber."

10 The Persian's Story

As the men sat in the torture chamber, the Persian began to explain how he met Erik and why he was so eager to help Raoul.

"I first met Erik in my country of Persia. He was a talented architect and was known to have an evil mind. He had been hired to build a torture chamber for the wicked Sultan of Mazenderan. When the chamber was finished, the sultan ordered Erik's death. As a policeman, I was to carry out the order. I knew Erik was a killer, but I felt sorry for him. Because of his ugliness, he had led a sad life. So I took him to the border and let him go. I gave him his life in return for a promise to disappear and to change his evil ways.

"Years later I saw Erik again in Paris, at the Opera house which he had helped design. He told me about his house on the lake in the cellar. I became interested in his project. I begged Erik to show me this house, but he acted strange and refused. So I followed him to see where he went. One day when I thought I was alone, I went down to the fifth cellar and found the lake. I got into Erik's boat and rowed toward the house.

"When I was in the middle of the lake, I was suddenly surrounded by a hushed voice that sang. It rose softly from the water. I leaned over the boat to listen. The water was perfectly calm and black as ink. Suddenly two strong arms rose up out of the water. They grabbed me by the neck and pulled me down. I would certainly have drowned if I had not cried out. Erik recognized my voice and pulled me to the bank.

"He said, 'How foolish you are to try to enter my house! I never invited you! I don't want you or anybody else there. Did you save my life just to make it unbearable?'

"He had almost killed me. I reminded him of his promise — no more murders.

"'Have I murdered anyone?' he asked with a friendly look.

"'Remember, you owe your life to me, Erik. What about the chandelier in the theater?'

"'Oh,' he laughed, 'that wasn't me! The chandelier was very old and worn. It fell by itself! Now, take my advice. Never again get in my boat, and never again try to enter my house!'

"From that day on, I gave up on the lake. But I knew there was another entrance to his house. So I followed him. I heard the music that made Christine so happy. Soon I found out about her relationship with Erik. Still I would never have thought that his voice could make her forget his ugliness. Hiding in her dressing room, I discovered the revolving mirror. It was then that I knew she had only heard the voice and had not seen the face.

"Then one day I found the monster with Christine in the cellar. She had obviously fainted. They were by the well, and a white horse was waiting beside them. I showed myself. It was terrible. Erik was furious. Sparks flew from his yellow eyes. Before I could speak, he hit me on the head. When I awoke, they were gone. I was sure the poor girl was his prisoner in the house at the lake. I went there and waited. I wanted Erik to see me. After a very long time he came out. 'You've been out here 24 hours,' he said. 'You are annoying me. I warn you this will end very badly. And it will be your fault. Forget about me! That's all I have to say. Unless you are a fool, it should be enough.'

"I could not stop worrying about Christine as his prisoner. I had often seen Erik disappear in the third cellar. So I went there and waited for hours behind some scenery. At last my patience was rewarded. Erik came toward me on his knees. He touched a spring on the wall, and a stone moved. He crawled through the hole it made in the wall.

"I saw Christine come and go from the house. I listened through the walls, and I learned the truth. Erik controlled her mind, but her heart belonged only to you, Raoul. I saw you two together when Erik let Christine go. You never suspected that anyone was watching over you. I would have killed the monster to protect you, but Erik never showed himself above the trapdoors.

"I went often to the stone's hole to listen. One day I heard amazing music. Erik was working on *Don Juan Triumphant*. He stopped playing and walked around like a madman. 'It must be finished first! All finished!' he said.

"I was not sure what he meant, but I got very worried. I wasn't surprised when Christine disappeared. I was prepared to act on my own. Erik would only be thinking about Christine now. This would be the time to enter the house through the third cellar. But then I saw how upset you were, and I decided to take you with me. There was no time to explain everything. I knew Erik too well.

"I knew he had once lived in India, where he mastered a method of choking his victims. No one knew better than he how to throw the Punjab lasso. It would whistle through the air and catch its victim around the neck. With one turn of the wrist, Erik would tighten the lasso. That is why I always had you hold one arm up close to your head. With an arm in that position it would be impossible for him to throw the lasso the right way.

"Erik probably killed Joseph Buquet for coming too close to his house. Thinking a clever person might get too curious about the lasso, Erik probably went back to get it. That is why the rope disappeared.

"I knew Erik was capable of terrible inventions. Of these, the most horrible and dangerous was the torture chamber. This room that we sit in now is an exact copy of the torture chamber at Mazenderan. It was a six-cornered room. The walls were covered with mirrors, so there seemed no way out. An iron tree was in the corner—a tree with branches from which victims could be hung."

The Persian stopped talking very suddenly. He grabbed Raoul's arm and motioned him to be silent. Raoul was very nervous, and he wanted only to call out to Christine. Suddenly there was a noise to their left. It was the sound of a door opening and shutting. Then there was a moan.

"You must make your choice! The wedding music or the funeral music!" It was Erik's voice. "The funeral song is not at all happy. On the other hand, the wedding song is wonderful! You must make up your mind. My masterpiece, *Don Juan Triumphant*, is finished. Now I want to live like everyone else. I want a wife. I want to take

her out on Sundays. I've invented a mask that makes me look like everybody else. You'll be so happy! We'll sing, by ourselves, until we're exhausted. But you are crying! You are afraid of me! I am not bad. Love me and you'll see!"

The moans increased. They were coming from Erik himself. Christine seemed to be silent with horror. Suddenly there was a bell ringing.

"Who has come uninvited to the lake now?" Erik asked. "Wait for me. I must answer the bell." Erik's footsteps moved away. A door closed. Christine was alone.

Raoul called to her. "Christine," said Raoul. "We are here to save you!"

"I must be dreaming," Christine's soft voice replied. Then she whispered to Raoul and the Persian that Erik had gone mad. He was threatening to kill people if she did not agree to marry him. He had given her until 11 o'clock the next night to say yes or no. But if she refused, Erik said that everyone would be buried.

"Hush! I hear him coming back!" whispered Christine. "Go away quickly!"

"We cannot, even if we wanted to. We are trapped in the torture chamber," Raoul replied.

The sound of the monster's steps finished the conversation.

"You are staring at me because I am all wet. My dear, it's not my fault. He rang the bell. But he'll never ring again. And now I must play the funeral music for him," Erik said calmly.

The Persian knew then just how mad Erik had become. He had just murdered whoever it was that had come to the door. The Persian also knew that he had to stop Erik before someone else got hurt.

11 The Torture Chamber

When Raoul heard Erik's words, he could not hold back his anger. And he cried out.

"What's that sound?" asked Erik. "Did you hear that cry? Is someone else in the house?"

"A cry?" asked Christine. "I heard nothing. Who else could be in the house?"

The sound of Raoul's voice seemed to set off Erik's madness. "I don't like the way you said that, my dear. You're trembling! Are you lying? Is someone here, in the torture chamber?"

"There is no one, Erik!"

"Well, it won't take long to find out. Christine, would you like to see? Climb up the folding steps. Go and look. Tell me what you see. Up you go! Is anyone there?"

The room was suddenly flooded with light. Raoul and the Persian heard the sound of steps against the wall. And then they heard Christine's voice saying, "There is no one there, dear."

"Well, OK. Come down now, since there is no one there! How did you like the view?"

"Very much!" answered Christine. She tried to speak naturally. But Erik's voice became sharp and shrill, and then low and deadly calm.

"What did you see?" he demanded quietly.

"I saw a forest," replied Christine.

"Did you see branches? Places from which to hang? That is why I call it the torture chamber. But it's just a joke! I am so tired of it all! I want a nice quiet apartment with ordinary doors and windows. . . . With a wife in it to care for me. My dear little Christine, are you listening? Tell me you love me! . . . No, you don't love me, but you will! . . . One can get used to anything. . . if one wants to. I will entertain you, Christine. I am the world's greatest ventriloquist! . . . Listen! Here, I'll raise my mask a little. Watch my lips. You see, they are not moving!"

Erik made sounds that seemed to come from every direction. He was completely mad. "Where would you like the voice? In those boxes on the fireplace? Now it's in the box on the left. Now it's in Carlotta's throat. What does it say? It's Mr. Toad. I'm singing co-ack! Co-ack! Now it's in the ghost's chair saying Carlotta is singing tonight to bring the chandelier down! Where is Erik's voice now? It's in the torture chamber! Pity them that have a nose, a real nose, and come to sniff around! Ha, ha, ha!"

Erik's crazed voice was everywhere. Christine's quiet voice tried to get his attention. "Erik! The wall is getting very hot. It's burning!"

The monster laughed loudly. "Yes, Christine. It's coming from the forest next door. It is a tropical forest!"

At first, Christine's pleas could be heard amidst the laughter. Then there was silence.

With the ceiling lit up, the room seemed to blaze with fire. The Persian and Raoul could see the room more clearly now. The mirrors were broken here and there, as if someone had kicked at them to escape the heat. Raoul paced around like a madman.

The Persian tried to reassure him. "I will find the way out. We have time. I am familiar with most of Erik's tricks. Look. Touch the walls. See? We are in a little room, not a burning forest. Keep saying that to yourself. And we will leave as soon as we find the door."

The Persian promised Raoul that he would find the trick door in less than one hour. He asked Raoul to lay down quietly on the floor.

Then the Persian set to work. He examined every inch of each glass panel, in all directions. He searched for the weak point where he would find the spring to make the door turn.

Suddenly there was the roar of a lion close by.

"Oh," said Raoul. "That lion is very close. Do you see it? . . . There, through the trees?"

After the lion came the sound of a leopard. Then the buzzing of flies. The Persian explained that Erik was making all the noises. As the heat surrounded the two men, they became very thirsty. Raoul pointed to a spot on the wall.

"Water!" he whispered.

"It's a mirage," said the Persian. "It's not real." But Raoul did not listen. He dragged himself toward the spot on the wall. He not only saw the water, he heard it ripple.

Then the two men heard the rain. They put out their tongues and dragged themselves toward the sound. When they reached the mirror, they both licked it.

It was burning hot! They writhed in pain, and the Persian's foot touched the Punjab lasso. He jumped in fear. But then something else caught his eye. He grabbed Raoul's arm and dragged him toward the lasso. Near it, he noticed a groove in the floor. In the groove was a black-headed nail. The Persian had found the spring! He felt it. It yielded to his touch. A trapdoor opened, and cool air came up from the black hole below.

There was a stone staircase leading down into Erik's cellar. At the bottom there were barrels stacked neatly in two rows. Barrels of water! All were sealed. Raoul broke one open.

"What is this? This isn't water!"

The Persian stooped down to look. When he did, he threw the lantern away with such force it

broke and went out. The two men were now in total darkness. What the Persian had seen in Raoul's hands was gunpowder!

Suddenly it was clear what Erik had meant before. If Christine refused him, people would indeed be buried—buried under the Paris Opera house! Erik was going to blow up the entire place.

Time was critical. What time was it? Raoul thought his watch was still running, so he broke the glass to feel the hands in the darkness. It was nearly 11 o'clock. Erik had given Christine until that very hour to give him an answer. Could the final hour be at hand?

There were footsteps next door. Someone tapped on the wall. It was Christine. Erik had left her alone for a few minutes.

"What time is it, Christine?" Raoul asked.

"It is nearly 11 o'clock," Christine replied. "There are only five minutes until the final hour!"

The Persian told Christine about the barrels of gunpowder they had found.

She said, "Yes, Erik is quite mad! He tore off the mask, and his eyes shot out flames! He said, 'I give you five minutes. Here is the key that opens the two boxes on the mantel. In one is a scorpion; in the other a grasshopper. Make your choice before I return. If you choose the scorpion, that will mean yes. The grasshopper will mean no.' His last words were, 'Be careful of the grasshopper! It can hop very high!' "

Christine knew that the five minutes were almost gone. The Persian explained that the grasshopper must be connected to an electric current that would blow up the gunpowder. Christine heard Erik's voice saying, "If you won't free the scorpion, Christine, then I will free the grasshopper!"

"Erik," Christine shouted. "Look! I am freeing the scorpion!"

Something cracked, then hissed like a rocket. It came softly at first, then louder. It was more like a gurgle now.

Raoul and the Persian rushed to the trapdoor. Water began to rise in the cellar. Without thinking the men bent down and drank. They went up the stairs and drank some more. But then they realized that the water was not stopping. There was enough to flood the whole house. Instead of burning, they would drown!

"Erik!" the Persian cried. "Turn off the tap!"

"Christine! Christine!" Raoul shouted.

Now the two men lost their footing. They spun around in the water and crashed against the mirrors. They clung to a branch of the tree, but had to release it. The water rose higher and higher. They choked and fought the dark water. They lost strength. The walls were too slippery. They began to sink.

One last effort! One last cry, "Erik! Christine!"

12 The Ghost's Story

The Persian awoke to find himself lying on a bed. An angel and a devil watched over him. Christine Daaè moved silently about, carrying tea. The man in the mask brought a cup to the Persian. Raoul was still asleep on a sofa nearby.

"He awakened long before we knew if you were still alive," Erik said to the Persian. "He is well and sleeping. We won't disturb him. You are both saved now. And soon, I shall take you up to the surface. . . to please my wife."

The Persian fell back asleep. When he awoke again, he was in his own apartment. His servant Darius said that someone had propped him against the apartment door, then rang the bell and ran away.

A few days later the Persian regained his strength. He asked about the de Chagny brothers. Darius told him that Raoul had disappeared and Philippe was dead. His body had been found on the bank of the Opera lake. It was Philippe that Erik had killed for ringing the bell at the house on the lake.

The Persian told his story to the police, but they treated him like a madman. He thought the newspapers might be more interested in the story. Just as he was writing the final lines, Darius announced a visitor. It was Erik.

Erik was extremely weak, and he leaned against the wall to keep from falling. He removed his hat to reveal a pale forehead. The rest of his face was covered by a mask.

The Persian rose and greeted him coldly. "Murderer of Philippe de Chagny, what have you done with his brother and Christine Daaè?"

Erik was stunned by the direct attack. He dragged himself to a chair. He spoke in short phrases and gasped for breath.

"Persian, . . . Count Philippe was dead. . . when I found him. . . . It was an. . . accident. . . a very sad accident! . . . He fell. . . into the lake!"

"You lie!" shouted the Persian.

"I have not. . . come here to. . . talk about anyone. . . but to tell you. . . I am about to die."

"Where are Raoul and Christine?"

"I am going to die. . . ."

"Raoul and Christine?" the Persian repeated.

"Of love, Persian. . . I am dying. . . of love. That is how it is. . . . I loved her so! . . . I love her still, Persian. . . ."

The Persian shook Erik by the arm. "Will you tell me? Is she dead?"

"No! No! She is not dead! And no one shall ever hurt her. Why were you there with that young

Raoul? . . . You could have been killed. My word! She begged for his life. But I reminded her that she had chosen the scorpion. Now she was engaged to me!

"As for you, you have Christine to thank. She had agreed to be my wife only to save you. And him. I had to promise to take you both up to the surface. I took you and came back alone. . . ."

"What did you do with Raoul?" interrupted the Persian.

"He was my hostage. But I couldn't keep him at the house because of Christine. So I locked him up in a dungeon in a cellar.

"When I came back, Christine was waiting. She was my real, living bride. She did not run away. She stayed. . . . She waited for me. . . . She even held out her forehead. I. . . I kissed her! . . . My happiness was so great, I cried. I ripped off my mask. . . and she did not run away! . . . And she did not die! . . . We wept together. . . . I have tasted all the happiness the world can offer.

"I had in my hand the plain gold ring I had given her. She had lost it, and I found it again. I gave it to her and said, 'This is my wedding gift. I know you love the boy.' I told her I knew I was only a poor dog to her. I said she should marry the young man.

"I brought him to Christine. She put on my ring and vowed to come back when I died. She

90

promised to bury me in secret, with the ring. I told her where to find my body. She knows what to do. Then she kissed me for the first time. Here on my forehead. If Christine keeps her promise, Persian, she will come back soon."

The Persian asked no more questions. He did not doubt what Erik had just said.

The monster collected his energy to leave. He promised to send something in gratitude.

Before he left, Erik answered the Persian's question about the two young people. He said that they had gone to find a priest. Then they went to some lonely spot where they could hide their happiness from the public.

Erik asked the Persian to inform the young couple of his death and to advertise it in the newspaper.

That was all. The Persian saw him to the door. Darius put him in a cab and said to the driver, "Take this gentleman to the Opera."

Three weeks later, the newspaper printed a notice: "Erik is dead."

Epilogue

Now you see why I know the Opera ghost was real. This case was very exciting—kidnapping, deaths, and disappearances.

What became of the singer Christine Daaè? The newspapers portrayed her as the victim of an argument between brothers. No one knew that she and Raoul disappeared to enjoy their happiness alone. They did not want it made public after the strange death of Philippe. They took a train north, that is all I know. Perhaps one day I'll look around Scandinavia for some trace of them. And also of Mrs. Valérius, who disappeared at the same time.

I am grateful to the Persian, who helped me daily. He gave me his papers and told me his memories of the Opera house. He sent me to people who had information he did not.

I was not able to find Erik's house. But in a dungeon in the Opera house I did find initials carved in the wall. Among them were R.C.: Raoul de Chagny. The letters are still there.